Picture Book

of

MOTHER GOOSE

This book belongs To: ....
....
....
....

Affectionately dedicated
TO BLIX
for whom so many of
these drawings were made

Song arrangements that begin on page 62 are reprinted from
Songs The Children Love To Sing published by D. Appleton and Company.
Used by permission of the publisher.

This 1987 edition is published by Derrydale Books,
distributed by Crown Publishers, Inc., 225 Park Avenue South, New York, New York 10003,
by arrangement with Horner/Stuart Enterprises

Printed and Manufactured in Hong Kong of America

Library of Congress Cataloging-in-Publication Data

Hader, Berta.
Picture book of Mother Goose.

Includes index.
Summary: A collection of Mother Goose rhymes
categorized under rhymes and songs, game songs, boys
and girls, and lullabies.
1. Nursery rhymes.   2. Children's poetry.
[1. Nursery rhymes]   I. Hader, Elmer, 1889–
II. Title.
PZ8.3.H117Pi   1987   87-8983
ISBN 0-517-64296-4
h g f e d c b a

Picture Book of Mother Goose

DERRYDALE BOOKS
NEW YORK

By Berta and Elmer Hader

TWINKLE, TWINKLE, LITTLE STAR

CONTENTS

CONTENTS CONTINUED

OLD MOTHER GOOSE

Old Mother Goose when
    She wanted to wander,
Would ride through the air
    On a very fine gander.

WILLY BOY, WILLY BOY

"Willy boy, Willy boy, where
    are you going?
I will go with you, if I may."

"I'm going to the meadow, to see
    them a-mowing,
I'm going to help them make the hay."

HARVEST HOME, HARVEST HOME

Harvest Home, harvest home,
Ne'er a load's been overthrown.

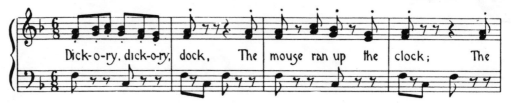

DICKORY, DICKORY, DOCK

Dick-o-ry, dick-o-ry, dock, The mouse ran up the clock; The clock struck "one", The mouse ran down; Dick-o-ry, dick-o-ry, dock.

Dickory, dickory, dock,
   The mouse ran up the clock,
The clock struck three,
   The mouse ran away,
Dickory, dickory, dock.

Dickory, dickory, dock,
   The mouse ran up the clock,
   The clock struck ten,
   The mouse came again,
Dickory, dickory, dock.

As I went to Bonner,
I met a pig
Without a wig—
Upon my word and honor.

THE COCK'S ON THE WOOD PILE

The cock's on the wood pile
    a-blowing on his horn,
The bull's in the barn
    a-threshing of corn,
The maids in the meadow
    are making of hay,
The ducks in the river
    are swimming away.

HICKETY PICKETY

Hickety Pickety, my little black hen
She lays eggs for gentlemen;
Sometimes nine, and sometimes ten
Hickety Pickety, my fat hen.

7

I LOVE LITTLE PUSSY

I love little Pussy,
   Her coat is so warm,
And if I don't hurt her,
   She'll do me no harm.

I'll sit by the fire
   And give her some food,
And Pussy will love me,
   Because I am good.

POLLY, PUT THE KETTLE ON

Polly, put the kettle on,
Polly, put the kettle on,
Polly, put the kettle on,
    And let's drink tea.

Sukey, take it off again,
Sukey, take it off again,
Sukey, take it off again,
    They're all gone away.

LITTLE GIRL, LITTLE GIRL, WHERE HAVE YOU BEEN?

"Little girl, little girl, where have you been?"
"Gathering roses to give to the Queen."
"Little girl, little girl, what gave she you?"
"She gave me a diamond as big as my shoe."

WHAT'S THE NEWS OF THE DAY?

What's the news of the day,
Good neighbor, I pray?
They say the balloon
Is gone up to the moon.

PIPE, CAT; DANCE, MOUSE

A cat came fiddling out of a barn,
With a pair of bagpipes under her arm;
She could sing nothing but "Fiddle cum fee,
The mouse has married the bumble bee."
Pipe, cat; dance, mouse;
We'll have a wedding at our good house.

LITTLE ROBIN REDBREAST

Little Robin Redbreast
    sat upon a tree,
Up went Pussy-cat and
    down went he;
Down came Pussy-cat and
    away Robin ran;
Says little Robin Redbreast,
    "Catch me if you can."

BAA, BAA, BLACK SHEEP

Baa, baa, black sheep,
    Have you any wool?
Yes, sir; yes, sir!
    Three bags full:

One for my master,
    One for my dame,
But none for the little boy
    Who cries in the lane.

BARBER, BARBER, SHAVE A PIG

Barber, barber, shave a pig,
How many hairs will make a wig?
"Four and twenty, that's enough."
Give the poor barber a pinch of snuff.

SMILING GIRLS, ROSY BOYS

Smiling girls, rosy boys,
Come and buy my little toys—
Monkeys made of gingerbread,
And sugar-horses painted red.

15

A DOG AND A CAT WENT OUT

A dog and a cat went out together
To see some friends just out of town,
Said the cat to the dog,
"What d'ye think of the weather?"
"I think, ma'am, the rain will come down;
But don't be alarmed, for I've an umbrella
That will shelter us both," said this amiable fellow.

A CROOKED MAN

There was a crooked man, and he went a crooked mile,
And he found a crooked sixpence against a crooked stile;
He bought a crooked cat, which caught a crooked mouse,
And they all lived together in a little crooked house.

PUSSY SITS BESIDE THE FIRE

Pussy sits beside the fire,
　　How did she come there?
In walks a little dog,
　　Says—"Pussy, are you there?

"How do you do, Mistress Pussy?
　　Mistress Pussy, how do you do?"
"I thank you kindly, little dog,
　　I fare as well as you."

THREE SISTERS IN A HALL

There were three sisters in a hall,
There came a knight amongst them all;
Good morrow, aunt, to the one,
Good morrow, aunt, to the other,
Good morrow, gentlewoman, to the third.

If you were my aunt,
    As the other two be,
I would say good morrow,
    The aunts, all three.

LITTLE BIRD

Once I saw a little bird
  Come hop, hop, hop;
So I cried, little bird,
  Will you stop, stop, stop?

And was going to the window
  To say How do you do?
But he shook his little tail,
  And far away he flew.

BLOW, WIND, BLOW

Blow, wind, blow! and go, mill, go!
That the miller may grind his corn;
That the baker may take it,
And into rolls make it,
And bring us some hot in the morn.

HICKORY, DICKORY, SACARA DOWN

Hickory, dickory, sacara down!
How many miles to Richmond town?
Turn to the left and turn to the right,
And you may get there by Saturday night.

THE NORTH WIND

Cold and raw the north wind doth blow,
Bleak in the morning early;
All the hills are covered with snow,
And winter's now come fairly.

POP! GOES THE WEASEL

All around the cobbler's bench
    the monkey chased the weasel;
The monkey thought 'twas all in fun,
    Pop! goes the weasel!

I've no time to wait or sigh,
    No patience to wait till by and by;
Kiss me quick I'm off, good-by,
    Pop! goes the weasel.

COBBLER, COBBLER

Cobbler, cobbler, mend my shoe,
   And get it done by half-past two:
If half-past two can't be done,
   Get it done by half-past one.

Cobbler, cobbler, mend my shoe,
   Give it a stitch and that will do:
Here's a nail and there's a prod,
   And now my shoe is well shod.

I SAW A SHIP A-SAILING

I saw a ship a-sailing,
   A-sailing on the sea;
And oh! it was all laden
   With pretty things for thee.

There were comfits in the cabin,
   And apples in the hold;
The sails were made of satin,
   And the masts were made of gold.

The four-and-twenty sailors
    That stood between the decks,
Were four-and-twenty white mice,
    With chains about their necks.

The captain was a duck, a duck,
    With a jacket on his back;
And when the ship began to move,
    The captain said, "Quack! Quack!"

POLL PARROT

Little Poll Parrot
    Sat in his garret,
Eating toast and tea;

A little brown mouse
    Jumped into the house,
And stole it all away.

OVER THE HILLS AND FAR AWAY

Tom, he was a piper's son,
He learnt to play when he
was young,
But all the tune that he
could play
Was "over the hills and
far away."

Tom with his pipe did play
with such skill
That those who heard him
could never keep still;
As soon as he played they
began for to dance,
Even pigs on their hind legs
would after him prance.

HOGS IN THE GARDEN

Hogs in the garden, catch 'em, Towser;
Cows in the cornfield, run, boys, run;
Cat's in the cream-pot, run, girls, run, girls;
Fire on the mountains, run, boys, run.

YOUNG LAMBS TO SELL

If I'd as much money as I could tell,
    I never would cry young lambs to sell;
Young lambs to sell, young lambs to sell;
    I never would cry young lambs to sell.

If I'd as much money as I could
    tell,
I never would cry old clothes
    to sell;
Old clothes to sell, old clothes
    to sell;
I never would cry old clothes
    to sell.

If I'd as much money as I could
    spend,
I never would cry old chairs
    to mend;
Old chairs to mend, old chairs
    to mend;
I never would cry old chairs
    to mend.

BOW, WOW, WOW!

Bow, wow, wow!
    Whose dog art thou?
Little Tommy Tinker's dog,
    Bow, wow, wow!

I'LL SING YOU A SONG

I'll sing you a song,
    Though not very long,
        Yet I think it as pretty as any;
            Put your hand in your purse,
          You'll never be worse,
            And give the poor singer a penny.

LITTLE DROPS OF WATER

Little drops of water,
　　Little grains of sand,
　　　Make the mighty ocean,
　　　　And the pleasant land.

33

ONE, TWO, THREE, FOUR, FIVE

One, two three, four, five,
  Once I caught a fish alive;
Six, seven, eight, nine, ten,
  I let him go again.

Why did you let him go?
  Because he bit my finger so;
Which finger did he bite?
  The little finger on the right.

THE COCK DOTH CROW

The cock doth crow to let you know,
    If you be wise, 'tis time to rise,
For early to bed and early to rise,
    Makes a man healthy and wealthy and wise.

SEE-SAW MARGERY DAW

See-saw Margery Daw,
Jacky shall have a new master;
Jacky must have but a penny a day,
Because he can work no faster.

GOOSEY, GOOSEY, GANDER

Goosey, goosey, gander,
   Where shall I wander?
Upstairs, downstairs,
   In my lady's chamber.
There I met an old man
   Who would not say his prayers;
I took him by the left leg,
   And threw him downstairs.

HEY, DIDDLE, DIDDLE!

Hey, diddle, diddle!
   The cat and the fiddle,
The cow jumped
   over the moon;
The little dog laughed
   to see such sport,
And the dish ran away
   with the spoon.

THREE WISE MEN OF GOTHAM

Three wise men of Gotham
They went to sea in a bowl,
And if the bowl had been stronger
My song had been longer.

HARK, HARK, THE DOGS DO BARK

Hark, hark, the dogs do bark!
Beggars are coming to town,
Some in rags, some in tags,
And some in velvet gown.

LAVENDER'S BLUE

Roses are red, lavender's blue;
If you will have me, I will have you.
Lilies are white, rosemary's green;
If you are king, I will be queen.

Call up your men, set them to work;
Some to the plough, some to the cart.
Some to make hay, some to cut corn;
Whilst you and I, keep ourselves warm.

LITTLE NUT TREE

I had a little nut tree, nothing would it bear
But a silver nutmeg and a golden pear;
The King of Spain's daughter came to visit me,
All on account of my little nut tree.

BURNIE BEE

Burnie bee, burnie bee,
Say, when will your wedding be?
If it be to-morrow day,
Take your wings and fly away.

THE OLD WOMAN AT THE TUB

The old woman must stand at the tub, tub, tub,
    The dirty clothes to rub, rub, rub;
But when they are clean and fit to be seen,
    I'll dress like a lady, and dance on the green.

PUSSY-CAT, PUSSY-CAT

Pussy-cat, pussy-cat, where
    have you been?
I've been to London to visit
    the queen.

Pussy-cat, pussy-cat, what
    did you there?
I frightened a little mouse
    under the chair.

SING A SONG OF SIXPENCE

Sing a song of sixpence,
  A pocket full of rye;
Four and twenty blackbirds
  Baked in a pie.
When the pie was opened,
  The birds began to sing;
Was not that a dainty dish,
  To set before the king?

The king was in the counting house
  Counting out his money;
The queen was in the parlour
  Eating bread and honey;
The maid was in the garden
  Hanging out the clothes,
Down came a blackbird,
  And pecked off her nose.

UP, UP, UP

Here we go up, up, up,
    And here we go down, down, downy,
      Here we go backward and forward,
        And here we go round, round, roundy.

HOT-CROSS BUNS

Hot-cross buns! Hot-cross
buns!
One a penny, two a penny,
Hot-cross buns!
If you have no daughters,
Give them to your sons,

One a penny, two a penny,
Hot-cross buns!
But if you have none of these little
elves,
Then you may eat them all your-
selves.

THERE WAS AN OWL

There was an owl lived in an oak,
  Whiskey, whaskey, weedle;
And all the words he ever spoke
  Were fiddle, faddle, feedle.

A sportsman chanced to come that way,
  Whiskey, whaskey, weedle;
Says he, "I'll shoot you, silly bird,
  So fiddle, faddle, feedle!"

OF ALL THE GAY BIRDS THAT E'ER I DID SEE

Of all the gay birds that e'er I did see,
The owl is the fairest by far to me:
For all the day long she sits in a tree,
And when the night comes, away flies she.

PAT A CAKE, PAT A CAKE

"Pat a cake, pat a cake,
  Baker's man."
"That I will, master,
  As fast as I can."
"Pat it and prick it,
  And mark it with a T,
And put it in the oven
  For Tommy and me."

RAIN, RAIN, GO AWAY

Rain, Rain, go away,
Come again another day,
Little Willie wants to play.

OLD WOMAN WHO LIVED IN A SHOE

There was an old woman who lived in a shoe,
She had so many children she didn't know what to do;
She gave them some broth without any bread,
And whipped them all well, and put them to bed.

VALENTINE, O VALENTINE

Valentine, O Valentine!
Curl your locks as I do mine;
Two before and two behind,
Good-morrow to you, Valentine.

THE ROSE IS RED,
THE VIOLET'S BLUE

The rose is red, the violet's blue,
The honey's sweet, and so are you.
Thou art my love, and I am thine,
I drew thee for my Valentine.
The lot was cast, and then I drew,
And fortune said it should be you.

OLD MOTHER HUBBARD

Old Mother Hubbard,
Went to the cupboard,
　To get her poor dog a bone,
But when she came there,
The cupboard was bare,
　And so the poor Dog had none.

She went to the baker's
　To buy him some bread,
But when she came back
　The poor dog was dead.

She went to the joiner's
　To buy him a coffin,
But when she came back
　The poor dog was laughing.

She took a clean dish
　　To get him some tripe,
But when she came back
　　He was smoking a pipe.

She went to the fruiterer's
　　To buy him some fruit,
But when she came back
　　He was playing the flute.

She went to the tavern
　　For white wine and red,
But when she came back
　　The dog stood on his head.

She went to the tailor's
　　To buy him a coat,
But when she came back
　　He was riding a goat.

She went to the barber's
　　To buy him a wig,
But when she came back
　　He was dancing a jig.

The Dame made a curtsy,
　　The dog made a bow;
The Dame said, "Your servant,"
　　The Dog said,

"Bow-wow."

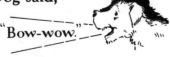

TWINKLE, TWINKLE, LITTLE STAR

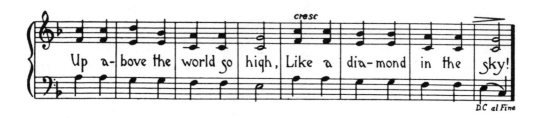

Twin-kle twin-kle lit-tle star; How I won-der what you are.

Up a-bove the world so high, Like a dia-mond in the sky!

2. When the blazing sun is gone,
    When he nothing shines upon,
    Then you show your little light,
    Twinkle, twinkle all the night.

3. Then the traveler in the dark,
    Thanks you for your tiny spark:
    How could he see where to go,
    If you did not twinkle so?

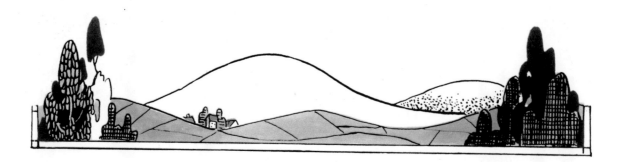

THE SOUTH WIND BRINGS WET WEATHER

The south wind brings wet weather,
The north wind wet and cold together,
The west wind always brings us rain,
The east wind blows it back again.

I SEE THE MOON AND THE MOON SEES ME

I see the moon and the moon sees me;
God bless the moon and God bless me.

THERE WAS A LITTLE WOMAN, AS I'VE BEEN TOLD

There was a little woman, as I've been told
Who was not very young, nor yet very old;
Now this little woman her living got
By selling codlins, hot, hot, hot!

Games
to play
in the
Mother
Goose
Way

ROUND AND ROUND THE VILLAGE

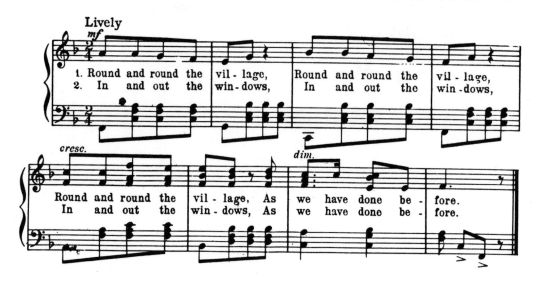

1. Round and round the vil-lage, Round and round the vil-lage,
2. In and out the win-dows, In and out the win-dows,

Round and round the vil-lage, As we have done be-fore.
In and out the win-dows, As we have done be-fore.

The children form a ring with one player on the outside, who runs around it while they are singing. During the second verse they raise their arms and let her in the center, and she runs in and out between the children, trying to complete the circle before the verse ends. In the third verse, she chooses her lover and they stand facing each other until the fourth verse when they exchange a kiss. Then the game begins all over again with the first child back in the circle and the one who was chosen as the lover on the outside.

LONDON BRIDGE

Allegretto

Lon - don bridge is fall-ing down, fall-ing down, fall-ing down

Lon - don bridge is fall-ing down, My fair la-dy.

2. Build it up with iron bars,
   Iron bars, iron bars,
   Build it up with iron bars,
   My fair lady.

3. Iron bars will bend and break,
   Bend and break, bend and break,
   Iron bars will bend and break,
   My fair lady.

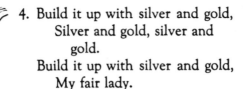

4. Build it up with silver and gold,
   Silver and gold, silver and
   gold.
   Build it up with silver and gold,
   My fair lady.

The children pass under a bridge formed by two children raising their arms to form an arch. These two children have previously secretly decided which one represents "gold" and which one "silver." At the words "My fair lady," the bridge falls—that is, the children imitating it, drop their hands—and the child who is caught is asked which it prefers, "gold or silver." This child then takes its place behind the one who represents his choice and the game continues until all have chosen. Then a tug-of-war between "gold and silver" ends the game.

ITISKIT, ITASKET

Not too fast

1. I-tis-kit, I-tas-ket, Green and yel-low bas-ket, I
wrote a let-ter to my love, And on the way I dropped it, I
dropped it, I dropped it, And on the way I dropped it.

A game similar in action to "drop the handkerchief." When the words are sung "I lost it" a letter or hand-kerchief is dropped behind some child by another who runs around the circle of players. This child picks it up and drops it behind some other child, and this keeps up until every child has had the handkerchief or letter.

THE FARMER IN THE DELL

Allegretto
mf

1. The farm-er in the dell, The farm-er in the dell,

f

dim.

Heigh-o! the der-ry oh, The farm-er in the dell.

2. The farmer takes a wife, etc.

3. The wife takes the child, etc.

4. The child takes the nurse, etc.

5. The nurse takes the dog, etc.

6. The dog takes the cat, etc.

7. The cat takes the rat, etc.

8. The rat takes the cheese, etc.

9. The cheese stands alone, etc.

A child, representing the farmer stands in the center of a circle of children, and chooses another child, "the wife" at the end of the second verse; this one chooses another, "the child," and so on until "the cheese" is selected, after which the game begins over again.

THE MUFFIN MAN

Moderato

1. O do you know the muf-fin man, The muf-fin man, the
2. O yes, I know the muf-fin man, The muf-fin man, the

muf-fin man, O do you know the muf-fin man, That lives in Dru-ry Lane?
muf-fin man, O yes, I know the muf-fin man, That lives in Dru-ry Lane.

The children form a circle, with one or more in the center; those in the circle dance around those in the center, singing the first verse; then they stand still while those in the center sing the second verse, afterward choosing others to join them in the center, and continuing to ask the question, until all have been chosen, and they all sing together, "We all of us know the Muffin Man," etc.

THE MULBERRY BUSH

Here we go round the mulberry bush, the mulberry bush, the mulberry bush,

Here we go round the mulberry bush, so early in the morning.

2. This is the way we iron our
   clothes, etc.
   So early Tuesday morning.

3. This is the way we scrub the
   floor, etc.
   So early Wednesday morning.

4. This is the way we mend our
   clothes, etc.
   So early Thursday morning.

5. This is the way we sweep the
   house, etc.
   So early Friday morning.

6. This is the way we bake our
   bread, etc.
   So early Saturday morning.

7. This is the way we go to church,
   etc.
   So early Sunday morning.

The game consists in simply suiting the actions to the words of each verse of the song. It is especially attractive for little girls.

MISS JENNY JONES

1. We've come to see Miss Jen-ny Jones, Miss Jen-ny Jones, Miss Jen-ny Jones, We've
   Miss Jen-ny is a-wash-ing, a-wash-ing, a-wash-ing, Miss

come to see Miss Jen-ny Jones, And how is she to-day?___
Jen-ny is a-wash-ing, You can't see her to-day.___

CHORUS

We're right glad to hear___ it, to hear___ it, to hear___ it,
      sorry

We're right glad to hear___ it, And how is she to-day?___
      sorry

2. Miss Jenny is a-starching, etc.

3. Miss Jenny is a-ironing, etc.

4. Miss Jenny is a-sweeping, etc.

5. Miss Jenny is a-sick-a-bed, etc.

6. Miss Jenny is a-dying, etc.

7. Miss Jenny is a-dead, etc.

One child represents Miss Jenny Jones, and another child her mother. The players dance in a circle around them, singing the verse "We've Come to See Miss Jenny Jones" and the two children in the center sing the answer "Miss Jenny is a-washing" etc. When the mother says "Jenny is dead," the children run away in all directions crying. The first one she catches takes her place in the center of circle and the game begins over again.

LAZY MARY

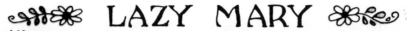

Allegro

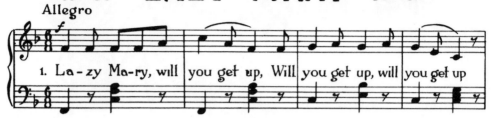

1. La-zy Ma-ry, will you get up, Will you get up, will you get up

La-zy Ma-ry, will you get up, Will you get up to-day?___

2. No, no, mother, I won't get up,   No, no, mother, I won't get up,
    I won't get up, I won't get up,   I won't get up to-day!

All the children sing the first verse, while dancing around the child chosen to be "Lazy Mary." Then they all sing the second verse together.

76

♔ THE KING OF FRANCE ♔

1. The King of France with for-ty thousand men, March'd up the hill and then march'd down again.
2. The King of France with for-ty thousand men, ___ Gave sa-lute and then march'd down again.

Two rows of children are formed, each with a leader and each facing the other. Each leader advances several steps singing and suiting their gestures to the words of the song. Then the two rows march toward each other, singing and imitating their leaders.

☙ TEN LITTLE INDIANS ☙

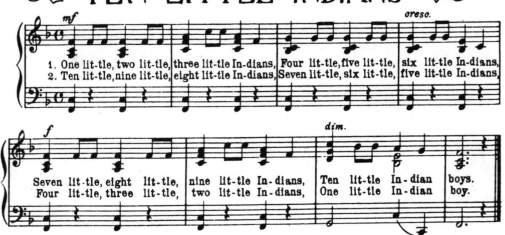

1. One lit-tle, two lit-tle, three lit-tle In-dians, Four lit-tle, five lit-tle, six lit-tle In-dians,
2. Ten lit-tle, nine lit-tle, eight lit-tle In-dians, Seven lit-tle, six lit-tle, five lit-tle In-dians,

Seven lit-tle, eight lit-tle, nine lit-tle In-dians, Ten lit-tle In-dian boys.
Four lit-tle, three lit-tle, two lit-tle In-dians, One lit-tle In-dian boy.

While singing the first verse, the children appear suddenly one by one, hopping Indian fashion. In the second verse they disappear one by one in the same way.

RING AROUND A ROSY

Ring a-round a ro - sy, Sit up-on a po - sy,

All the girls in our town vote for Un-cle Jo - sy.

All the players dance around in a ring, and fall down at the last words.

LITTLE SALLY WATERS

Moderato

mf

Lit-tle Sal-ly Wa-ters, sit-ting in the sun, Cry-ing and

weep-ing—— for—— a young man. Rise, Sal-ly, rise,

wipe off your eyes, Fly to the East, fly to the

West, Fly to the ve-ry one that you love best.

The children form a ring, with the child representing "Sally Waters" in the center. She kneels or sits on the ground, with her face in her hands as if weeping. The ring of children dance round singing the verse; and at the words "Rise, Sally Rise," she rises and chooses another from the ring who goes into the center with her. She then joins the ring and the other child takes her place. The game continues until each child has taken the part of Sally Waters.

GIRLS AND BOYS COME OUT TO PLAY

Girls and boys come out to play, The moon doth shine as bright as day

Come with a whoop and come with a call, And come with a good will or not at all.

This is a kind of "free-for-all" game in which the children join hands in a circle to frolic and dance to their heart's content.

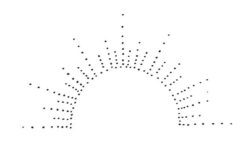

Boys and girls from Mother Goose

GEORGIE PORGIE

Allegretto

Geor-gie Por-gie, pud-ding and pie, Kiss'd the girls and made them cry;

When the girls came out to play, Geor-gie Por-gie ran a-way

LITTLE BO-PEEP

Little Bo-Peep has lost her sheep,
  And can't tell where to find
    them;
Leave them alone, and they'll come
    home,
  And bring their tails behind
    them.

Little Bo-Peep fell fast asleep,
  And dreamt she heard them
    bleating;
But when she awoke, she found it
    a joke,
  For they still were all fleeting.

Then up she took her little crook,
  Determined for to find them;
She found them indeed, but it
    made her heart bleed,
  For they'd left all their tails
    behind 'em.

It happened one day, as Bo-Peep
    did stray
  Into a meadow hard by;
There she espy'd their tails, side by
    side,
  All hung on a tree to dry.

She heaved a sigh, and wiped her
    eye,
  Then went over hill and dale, O!
And tried what she could, as a
    shepherdess should,
  To tack to each sheep its tail, O!

91

THERE WAS A LITTLE GIRL, AND SHE WORE A LITTLE CURL

There was a little girl, and she wore
    a little curl
Right down the middle of her
    forehead;

When she was good, she was very,
    very good,
But when she was bad she was
    horrid.

HERE AM I, LITTLE JUMPING JOAN

Here am I, little jumping Joan;
When nobody's with me,
   I'm always alone.

HANDY-SPANDY

Handy-Spandy, Jack-a-dandy,
Loved plum-cake and sugar-candy.
He bought some at a grocer's shop,
And out he came, hop, hop, hop.

MARY HAD A LITTLE LAMB

Mary had a little lamb,
    Its fleece was white as snow;
And everywhere that Mary went
    The lamb was sure to go.

It followed her to school one day,
    That was against the rule;
It made the children laugh and
      play,
    To see a lamb at school.

And so the teacher turned it out,
    But still it lingered near;
And waited patiently about
    Till Mary did appear.

"Why does the lamb love Mary
    so?"
    The eager children cry;
"Why, Mary loves the lamb, you
    know!"
    The teacher did reply.

LITTLE TOMMY TUCKER

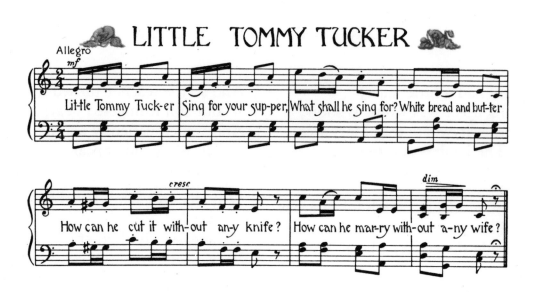

Lit-tle Tommy Tuck-er | Sing for your sup-per, | What shall he sing for? | White bread and but-ter

How can he cut it with-out an-y knife? | How can he mar-ry with-out a-ny wife?

DEEDLE DEEDLE, DUMPLING

Deedle, deedle, dumpling, my son John,
He went to bed with his stockings on,
One shoe off, and one shoe on,
Deedle, deedle, dumpling, my son John.

ELSIE MARLEY

Elsie Marley is grown so fine,
She won't get up to serve the swine,
But lies in bed till eight or nine,
And surely she does take her time.

And do you ken Elsie Marley, honey?
The wife who sells the barley, honey?
She won't get up to serve her swine,
And do you ken Elsie Marley, honey?

TOM, TOM, THE PIPER'S SON

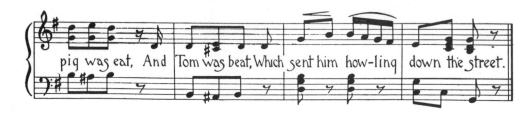

Tom, Tom, the pi-per's son, Stole a pig, and a-way he run! The

pig was eat, And Tom was beat, Which sent him how-ling down the street.

LITTLE BOB SNOOKS

Little Bob Snooks was
    fond of his books,
And loved by his usher
    and master;
But naughty Jack Spry, he
    got a black eye,
And carries his nose in
    a plaster.

LITTLE BOY BLUE

Little Boy Blue, come, blow up
    your horn,
The cow's in the meadow, the
    sheep's in the corn.

But where is the little boy tending
    the sheep?
He's under the haycock fast asleep.

LITTLE JACK HORNER

Little Jack Horner
Sat in a corner,
Eating of Christmas pie;
    He put in his thumb,
    And pulled out a plum,
And cried, "What a good
      boy am I!"

LITTLE TEE WEE

Little Tee Wee,
He went to sea,
In an open boat;
And while afloat
The little boat bended,
And my story's ended.

JACK BE NIMBLE

Jack be nimble,
And Jack be quick,
And Jack jump over
The candlestick.

MISTRESS MARY

Mistress Mary,
Quite contrary,
How does your garden grow?
With silver bells,
And cockleshells,
And pretty maids all in a row.

BOBBY SHAFTO HAS GONE TO SEA

Bobby Shafto has gone to sea,
With silver buckles at his knee;
When he comes back he'll marry
    me,—
  Bonny Bobby Shafto!

A DILLER, A DOLLAR

A diller, a dollar,
A ten o'clock scholar;
What makes you come so soon?
You used to come at ten o'clock,
And now you come at noon.

CURLY LOCKS

Cur-ly locks! Cur-ly locks! wilt thou be mine? thou shalt not wash dishes nor yet feed the swine; But

sit on a cush-ion and sew a fine seam, And feast up-on strawberries, sugar and cream

BILLY, BILLY

"Billy, Billy, come and play,
    While the sun shines bright as day."
"Yes, my Polly, so I will,
    For I love to please you still."

"Billy, Billy, have you seen
    Sam and Betsy on the green?"
"Yes, my Poll, I saw them pass,
    Skipping o'er the new-mown grass."

JACK AND JILL

Jack and Jill went up the hill
　To fetch a pail of water;
Jack fell down and broke his crown
　And Jill came tumbling after.

Up Jack got and home did trot
　As fast as he could caper;

Went to bed and bound his head
　With vinegar and brown paper.

When Jill came in how she did grin
　To see Jack's paper plaster;
Mother vexed, did whip her next
　For causing Jack's disaster.

SIMPLE SIMON

Simple Simon met a pieman
  Going to the fair;
Says Simple Simon to the pieman,
  "Let me taste your ware."

Says the pieman to Simple Simon,
  "Show me first your penny";
Says Simple Simon to the pieman,
  "Indeed, I have not any."

Simple Simon went to look
    If plums grew on a thistle;
He pricked his fingers very much,
    Which made poor Simon whistle.

He went to catch a dickey-bird,
    And thought he could not fail,
Because he'd got a little salt
    To put upon its tail.

He went to shoot a wild duck,
    But wild duck flew away;
Says Simon, "I can't hit him,
    Because he will not stay."

Simple Simon went a-fishing
    For to catch a whale;
All the water he had got,
    Was in his mother's pail.

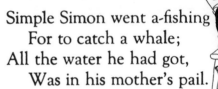
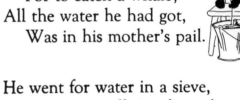

He went for water in a sieve,
    But soon it all ran through;
And now poor Simple Simon
    Bids you all adieu.

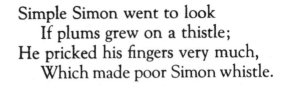

He went to slide upon the ice,
    Before the ice would bear;
Then he plunged in above his knees,
    Which made poor Simon stare.

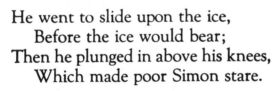

113

LITTLE BETTY BLUE

Little Betty Blue
Lost her holiday shoe,
What can little Betty do?
Give her another,
To match the other,
And then she may walk in two.

LUCY LOCKET

Lucy Locket lost her pocket,
Kitty Fisher found it;
There was not a penny in it,
But a ribbon round it.

POLLY FLINDERS

Little Polly Flinders
Sat among the cinders,
   Warming her pretty little toes!
Her mother came and caught her,
And whipped her little daughter,
   For spoiling her nice new clothes.

HERE'S SULKY SUE

Here's Sulky Sue;
   What shall we do?
Turn her face to the wall
   Till she comes to.

WEE WILLIE WINKIE

Wee Willie Winkie runs through
    the town,
Upstairs and downstairs in his
    night-gown,

Rapping at the window, crying
    through the lock,
"Are the children all in bed for
    it's now eight o'clock?"

Some Lullabys to play and sing

CRADLE SONG

J. Brahms

1. Lul-la-by and good-night, with ro-ses be-dight, With li-lies be-
2. Lul-la-by and good-night, thy moth-er's de-light, Bright an-gels a-

decked is— ba-by's wee bed; Lay thee down now and rest, may thy
round my— dar-ling shall stand; They will guard thee from harms, thou shalt

slum-ber be blest, Lay thee down now and rest, may thy slumber be blest.
wake in my arms, They will guard thee from harms, thou shalt wake in my arms.

ROCK-A-BYE BABY

Andante

Rock-a-bye ba-by on the tree-top, when the wind blows the cra-dle will rock;

When the bough breaks the cra-dle will fall, Down will come ba-by, cra-dle and all.

2. Hush-a-by, baby on the tree-top,
When the wind blows the cradle
will rock.

3. When the bough breaks the cradle
will fall,
Down will come baby, cradle and all.

DANCE A BABY DIDDY

Allegretto

1. Dance a ba - by did - dy, What can mam-my do wid-'e?___
2. Dance, my ba - by dear - ie, Ma will nev - er be wea - ry,___

Sit in her lap. Give it some pap, And dance a ba - by did - dy.
Fro - lic and play, Now while you may, So dance, my ba - by dear - ie.___

TO BABYLAND

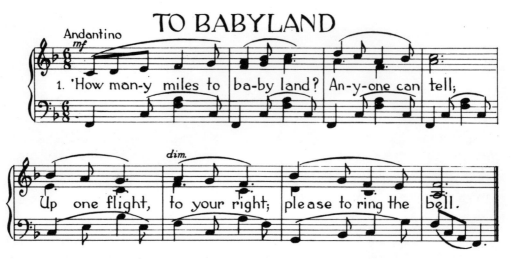

Andantino
mf

1. 'How man-y miles to ba-by land? An-y-one can tell;

dim.

Up one flight, to your right; please to ring the bell.

2. What do they do in baby land?
     Dream and wake and play;
   Laugh and crow, fonder grow,
     Jolly times have they.

3. What do they say in babyland?
     Why, the oddest things;
   Might as well try to tell
     What a birdie sings.

4. Who is the queen in baby land?
     Mother, kind and sweet;
   And her love born above,
     Guides the little feet.

CRADLE SONG

C. M. Von Weber

Moderato

1. Sleep, my heart's dar-ling, in slum-ber re-pose; Let the fair
2. Now, dear-est ba-by, is morn's gold-en time; Not thus thou'lt

lids o'er those blue eyes now close, All is as peace-ful and
slum-ber in life's lat-er prime; Sor-row and care then will

cresc. *dim*

still as the tomb, Nor shall the gnats wake thee with their low hum.
watch by thy bed. Ne'er more sweet peace will there pil-low thy head.

BABY BUNTING

Allegretto

Bye, Ba—by Bunt—ing, Dad—dy's gone a —hunt — ing, To

get a lit — tle rab—bit skin, To wrap his Ba—by Bunt—ing in.

SLEEP O SLEEP

Andantino

1. Sleep, O sleep!__ While breez-es so soft-ly are blow-ing;
2. Sleep, O sleep!__ While birds in the for-ests are sing-ing;
3. Sleep, O sleep!__ While an-gels are watch-ing be-side thee;

Sleep, O sleep!__ While stream-lets so gent-ly are flow-ing,
Sleep, O sleep!__ While ech-oes with mu-sic are ring-ing,
Sleep, O sleep!__ May bless-ings for-ev-er be-tide thee,

Sleep, O sleep!__ Sleep,__ O__ sleep!
Sleep, O sleep!__ Sleep,__ O__ sleep!
Sleep, O sleep!__ Sleep,__ O__ sleep!

I WILL SING A LULLABY

1. Gold-en slumbers kiss your eyes, Smiles a-wake you when you rise, Sleep, pretty lov'd ones do not cry, And I will sing a lul-la-by, Lul-la-by, lul-la-by, lul - la-by.—

2. Care is heavy, therefore sleep,
    You are care, and care must keep;
Sleep, pretty lov'd ones, do not cry,
    And I will sing a lullaby,
Lullaby, lullaby, lullaby.—

132

SLEEP BABY SLEEP

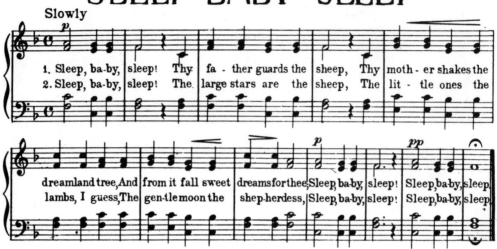

Slowly

1. Sleep, ba-by, sleep! Thy fa - ther guards the sheep, Thy moth - er shakes the
2. Sleep, ba-by, sleep! The large stars are the sheep, The lit - tle ones the

dreamland tree, And from it fall sweet dreams for thee, Sleep ba-by, sleep! Sleep, ba-by, sleep.
lambs, I guess, The gen-tle moon the shep-herdess, Sleep, ba-by, sleep! Sleep, ba-by, sleep.

BED TIME

Not too fast

1. The eve-ning is com-ing, The sun sinks to rest, The crows are all fly-ing straight home to the nest. "Caw" says the crow as he flies o-ver-head, "Its time lit-tle peo-ple were go-ing to bed!

2. The flowers are closing
   The daisy's asleep,
   The primrose is buried
   In slumber so deep,
   Closed for the night
   are the roses so red,
   It's time little people
   were going to bed!

3. The butterfly, drowsy,
   Has folded its wing;
   The bees are returning,
   No more the birds sing.
   Their labour is over,
   their nestlings are fed;
   It's time little people
   were going to bed!

THE SANDMAN COMES German Song

The Sand-man comes, the Sand-man comes, He has such pret-ty snow-white sand, and well he's known through-out the land, The Sand-man comes!

138

OUR BABY

1. Cheeks of rose, ti-ny toes, Has our lit-tle ba-by;
Eyes of blue, fin-gers too, Cun-ning all as may be.

2. Thee I love, sweetest dove,
   Darling little baby!

While I live, thee I'll give
Kisses warm as may be.

INDEX

143

FINIS.